Ultimate Success in the Game of Life

Tyrone Poole

ULTIMATE SUCCESS IN THE GAME OF LIFE
Copyright © 2011 by Tyrone Poole

All rights reserved. No part of this publication may be reproduced, stored in a retrieval system, or transmitted in any form by means electronic, mechanical, photocopying, recording or otherwise, except for the inclusion of brief quotations in a review, without prior permission in writing from the publisher.

ISBN: 978-0-9846515-1-1

Published by

LIFEBRIDGE
BOOKS
P.O. Box 49428
Charlotte, NC 28277

Printed in the United States of America.

Dedication

This book is dedicated to my wife, Jennifer, our children, Tyra, Nakai, and Tyson, and my parents RoseMary and Hilliard Poole. Also to Ashton Poole, Bishop Wiley Jackson, Jesse Heard, Eugene Coleman, Doug Porter, Bill Polian, Bill Belichick, Mike Shanahan, Eric Davis, Rob Ryan, the Carolina Panthers organization, the 1995 Carolina Panthers coaching staff, Fort Valley State University, and to everyone who believes that they are above and not beneath.

Contents

	Introduction	7
1	Who Wants a Quitter?	11
2	Life Beyond Church's Chicken	31
3	A Prayer That Came True	47
4	"This is What You are Playing For"	57
5	The Turn-Around	69
6	Be a Thoroughbred, Not a Donkey	83
7	Never Run From Reality	95
8	What Is Your Hot Sauce	109
9	Who Controls Your Future?	121
10	The Key to Ultimate Success	133

INTRODUCTION

Perhaps you've met those who don't believe success will ever be theirs. They look around and see people who come from better backgrounds, have more education, are taller, stronger, better looking, and wonder, "Why should I even try to compete? They have all the advantages."

What you are about to read will put all of these excuses to rest.

I want to share the story of a young man who came from the wrong side of the tracks—me. If anyone needed reasons to fail, I certainly could have written the list.

Even when I was finally making strides in the right direction, there came a point when I blew it all and my life came to a complete standstill.

How does a young man who did not finish his senior year of football, not only become a first-round draft pick in the NFL, but wind up with not just one Super Bowl ring, but *two*?

The reason for this book is not to simply recount my journey, but to share what I have learned along the way. In these chapters you will find 12 principles that are the foundation on which I have built my life. I like to call them "concrete shoes." In other words, they have provided a rock-solid footing for what I have been fortunate enough to accomplish.

They not only apply to sports, but to life itself.

You will learn:
- How to choose the right pattern to follow.
- Who to surround yourself with.
- How your words affect your actions.
- The tools you need for your journey.
- How to raise your bar of learning.
- The key to rising above defeat.
- The power of depending upon yourself.
- How to develop a "nothing but the best" philosophy.
- The secret of staying focused and never giving up.

Plus, I will share what I believe is the most important decision you will ever make. I was half way through my professional career before this dramatic turn-around happened to me—and it profoundly changed every aspect of my future.

After you have finished this book, let me encourage you to pass it along to a young person who is searching for direction and needs some guiding principles to chart their course. Together, we can impact their lives.

You're about to discover *Ultimate Success in the Game of Life.*

– Tyrone Poole

Chapter 1

Who Wants a Quitter?

It was the fall of 1989 and I was floating on top of the world.

Our football team, the "Grangers," at LaGrange High School in Georgia, was headed for another winning season and I was loving every minute under the Friday night lights at Callaway Stadium.

For two years I had been the starting tailback and was really feeling my oats. College scouts were in the crowd at all of our games and the players were already talking about the athletic scholarship they knew would be coming their way. I felt down deep in my heart I was about to be handed a free ride to an outstanding university.

Then, on an October afternoon during my senior

year, about half way through the season, I showed up late for practice. Was I ever in for a surprise!

Coach Guthrie, in front of the entire team, gave me a tongue-lashing I will never forget. Being young and immature, I didn't know he was using me, one of the leaders of the team, as an example. He was sending a strong message to the rest of the squad that if they broke the rules, there would be consequences.

All of a sudden, my ego kicked in. I was thinking, "Wait a minute. I'm a star! Why are you talking to me this way?"

That afternoon, I felt totally humiliated in front of my peers.

"TYRONE, IT'S OVER"

Looking back, I should have handled the situation far better, but I let my emotions get the best of me. With my teammates wondering how I would react, I took off my helmet, threw it defiantly to the turf, grit my teeth and began stomping off the field.

After a few steps, I expected coach Guthrie to yell, "Stop Tyrone. Come on back!"

The silence was deafening. Since I didn't hear

anything I kept walking. With every step I thought it would be like having a spat between boyfriend and girlfriend, you would apologize and make up.

This didn't happen. Coach Guthrie never uttered a word. So I headed straight to the locker room and waited there until practice was over and the rest of the team returned. I didn't have much of a choice since I needed a ride home from one of my buddies.

The rest of the players came in and circled around me. Some of them advised, "Tyrone, you need to apologize to the coach," and I really thought about it. But the following day, when I came back for the next workout, the coach walked over to me and said, "Tyrone, it's over. Don't come back to practice anymore."

I can't explain the gut-wrenching feeling in the pit of my stomach. It seemed that every dream I had of playing college football had suddenly been smashed to pieces.

I was heart-sick, but there was nothing I could do about it. The decision had been made.

It was painful to sit in the stands and watch our team during the rest of the season. With every fiber of my being, I wanted to be out on that field.

Then came the spring when several of my teammates were offered college football scholarships. But not Tyrone Poole.

Who wants a quitter?

The Other Side of the Tracks

Let me take you back a few years earlier to where it all began.

I discovered America in LaGrange, Georgia, an historic southern town of approximately 30,000 about an hour southwest of Atlanta, very close to the Alabama border.

It's a wonderful community that has a rich heritage, with classic antebellum homes like the Belleview Estate near downtown on Ben Hill Street.

———————— ⋙ ————————

The Poole family, however, lived on the other side of the tracks.

My dad, Hilliard, was a humble man about six-foot-one, who took whatever job was available at the time. He spent years as a cook, then worked for a Coca-Cola distributor until he had an on-the-job injury that left him on disability. He was an avid green-thumb gardener and every summer there would be a plot in our back yard yielding tomatoes, green beans, and other vegetables. That was his hobby until he passed away in 2005.

Mom, RoseMary, was a terrific homemaker, who pushed me to succeed and did her best to instill in me integrity, character, and positive values. I was their only child.

Later in her life, because of the lack of finances, my mother took a course in elderly care and found employment at a retirement home.

SUNDAYS AT BETHLEHEM

Regarding church, both of my parents came from a spiritual heritage. We were members of the Bethlehem Missionary Baptist Church, located on a country road near Five Points, Alabama, a stone's-throw across the Georgia state line. This is where my grandparents were married, buried, and held membership—a tradition we continued.

The church was a half-hour drive from our home in LaGrange, and even though we weren't in attendance every Sunday, my parents were faithful supporters of God's work. In addition to paying tithes, when the collection plate came around, mom would always give me fifty cents or a dollar to drop in.

At home, the Holy Scriptures were highly esteemed and talked about.

One of my earliest memories is of my father reading to me from a large picture-Bible. It made an indelible impression on my young life.

The Bethlehem church had an outdoor baptismal pool—which resembled an oversized hot tub.

One humid Sunday afternoon when I was seven, several of my cousins were being baptized and I wanted to join them.

At that young age I did not understand the full meaning of baptism, but as we stood together in that small pool, the pastor, Reverend William Trammell, spoke a few words. One by one, he lowered my cousins down into the water and raised them up. An assistant placed a white cloth over the shoulders of the newly baptized.

By the time it was my turn, my heart was fluttering like the wings of a hummingbird. I don't remember what the minister said, but I do know that when I came out of the water I felt washed and clean like a brand new person. It is a memory that is seared into my heart and mind.

Getting By

Some believe an only child is a spoiled child, but that certainly wasn't true of me.

———————— ✵ ————————

To say we lived in humble surroundings is an understatement.

Our small wood-frame home at 205 Euclid Avenue in the southeast part of town provided shelter, yet certainly not any luxuries. During the winter we would tape plastic around the windows to keep the heat trapped inside.

We owned two space-heaters, but to save money,

spent most of our time in one room and sealed off the others. It also helped when we put towels and blankets at the base of the doors so the frigid winds would not blow in.

After breakfast on cold mornings, my parents would always leave the oven door open so there would be a little extra blast of heat in the kitchen.

To escape the oppressive summer temperatures, we bought a window air-conditioning unit for the bedroom. Once again we would seal off the other rooms and stay where it was cool.

I was always hesitant to invite my friends inside our home because our only bathroom was in such poor shape. The shower didn't work, so we hooked up a garden hose to the kitchen sink, ran it out a window and into the bathroom window for a makeshift shower.

When it rained, some rooms of the house would leak. One specific area was in the living room, right over our radio-phonograph that played those old

45rpm vinyl records. To prevent any serious damage we placed a bucket on top of the radio to catch the drips.

An Extended Family?

In addition to my mom and dad, we had other residents living in our house—rats and roaches!

There were nights when we were relaxing, watching televison, and the audio was in real competition with the scratching sounds of mice crawling up and down in between the drywall and exterior siding. After a while it didn't even faze us—we felt like they were neighbors.

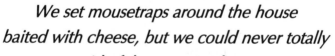

We set mousetraps around the house baited with cheese, but we could never totally get rid of the unwanted guests.

During the night, if I had to get up use the bathroom, when I turned on the light, the cockroaches would start scurrying for an exit. Those early times reminded me of the verse in the Bible where it talks about light clearing away the darkness. Well, it sure scared away the roaches!

Ours was a one-bedroom house, so when I was little I slept in the same bed as my mom and dad. But as I grew older I would make a palate on the floor or bunk down on the couch in our living room.

Finally, during my junior year of high school, dad saved enough money to hire a handyman to construct a small add-on bedroom. It was nothing special to look at—and so cramped I could touch the ceiling. There was barely enough room for a bed and the only air for the room was a fan we sat on the floor, but it was all mine.

We got by, yet it was not exactly a situation that was conducive for success. However, our home was filled with love—and I certainly had plenty of guidance and constructive criticism.

Lessons to Learn

From kindergarten on, I loved school, but was always the one getting into trouble. I talked when I was supposed to be quiet, and ran when the teacher told us not to.

I spent far too many hours warming a chair in the

principal's office and often had to stay after school for acting up. Because of this I'd miss the bus and have to run or jog to the bus stop in our neighborhood and meet up with the rest of the kids—so my parents wouldn't know what happened. I'm sure it improved my abilities in track!

Once, in the fourth grade, the teacher announced that we were going to make chocolate chip cookies for a home economics class. Each student was asked to bring a particular ingredient, and my item was the chocolate chips.

Upset because the teacher would not let me stir the chocolate chips, I told her I was going to take them home with me—and that's exactly what I did. Of course, I ate them during the bus ride!

I thought I had gotten away with something, but that feeling was short lived. The school had phoned my parents and told them about my stubbornness.

When I walked through the door, my dad really let me have it.

I learned a valuable lesson that day about cooperation.

Playground Practice

Athletically, I wasn't involved in any organized sports until I was in junior high school in the seventh and eighth grades. I developed a few skills, however, playing in the neighborhood with the other kids.

Without question, I developed plenty of speed playing Hide n' Go Seek. This is where you chose a home base such as the front porch or a tree, then one person covers their eyes and counts to ten while the other kids scramble to find a hiding place. If the person who is "it" finds you, they have to race you back to home base—but if they get there first you are out of the game.

———————— ⟫ ————————

*Since I hated losing, I became
a very fast runner.*

We tried everything—basketball, football, and softball (we played that with a tattered tennis ball since we couldn't afford a real softball). Sometimes we would just play "strike out" where you only have a pitcher and a batter.

One of my favorites was speedball. The object of the game is to throw, kick, or head the ball into a goal. We divided up into teams and played our hearts out, but it got rather serious at times.

The Dust Was Flying!

Since we didn't have a basketball goal at our house I decided to build my own. I scrounged around the neighborhood until I found an old 2x4 and nailed a piece of discarded plywood for the backboard. I located an old bicycle wheel and used an axe to get rid of the spokes. Then I put several nails through the spoke holes and into the backboard.

Wanting to make it as authentic as possible, I located some netting and used duck tape to hang it from the rim. Finally, I dug a hole in the ground in our backyard, stabilized the post with some rocks, covered it up with dirt and added wood braces at the bottom to keep it straight.

The grass in that area soon turned to red Georgia dirt, but my friends and I didn't mind the dust that was flying everywhere as we practiced.

At the playground, I loved doing pull-ups on the monkeys bars. Then one day I decided to build my muscles with weight lifting. Since we didn't have the money for equipment, I made my own barbell set by putting cinder blocks on each end of a discarded steel rod. It may sound primitive, but it certainly worked for me!

An Encouraging Word

There was one activity in elementary school I really enjoyed. Our fifth and sixth grade physical education teacher, coach Parson, would organize a wrestling tournament for the guys.

We would wrestle in the gym throughout the school year in different weight classes. And if you made it to the finals you got to wrestle in front of the whole school on the stage of the auditorium.

I managed to win my weight class for two years in a row. Coach Parson took me aside and encouraged me to think about pursuing sports when I entered junior high.

———————— ❧ ————————

In seventh grade, at the new school, I was in a class taught by a coach named Mr. Jackson. He also recognized some of the athletic abilities I evidently possessed.

One day as I was on my way home, I cut across the athletic fields trying to shorten my walk.

Spotting me, coach Jackson called out my name and asked me to come into the gym where they were conducting basketball tryouts for the team.

"I really haven't signed up for any sports," I told him.

"Don't worry about that," he responded—and he ended up picking me for his team.

In our junior high the teams had nicknames like the NBA professionals—the Celtics, the Lakers, the Pistons, etc. Ours was called the Supersonics.

I was a very good street-ball player but since it was my first encounter with organized sports I had a lot to learn. I was rather shy and reluctant to let my skills rise to the surface. In truth, I didn't understand the concept of team play because in the neighborhood it was pretty much every boy for himself!

I caught on, but it was a slow process.

"BULL IN THE RING"

High school was around the corner and the word about incoming freshmen had already filtered up to the coaches. My reputation was that I had plenty of raw talent and capabilities, but they needed to be sharpened, refined, and directed.

One of the ninth grade coaches talked my mom into letting me go out for football—which she wasn't exactly thrilled about. During my first high school year I wrestled, ran track, and played football.

I started out as a quarterback but couldn't seem to master the position. In practice, my tendency was to throw the ball as hard as I could—even if the receiver was only five yards in front of me. I really didn't have enough control, so the coaches moved me to tailback where I played much better.

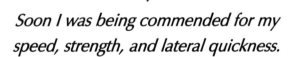

Soon I was being commended for my speed, strength, and lateral quickness.

However, my freshman year turned out to be a disaster. One afternoon in practice, the coach had us involved in a drill called "Bull in the Ring." This is where your teammates form a circle around you and the coach taps someone on the shoulder to attack you—shoulder-pad to shoulder-pad. Then another player attacks. You are like a hot potato with your feet moving fast and your eyes darting in all directions to see where the next charge is coming from.

Unfortunately, during one of those drills, I broke my ankle and had to sit out for the rest of the season.

My mom was actually relieved because she wasn't at all enthusiastic about me being involved in contact sports. Instead, she wanted me to end my football career right then. "You're not going back out there," she insisted.

My sophomore year was the same. No football.

It wasn't until my third year of high school that the coaches talked my parents into letting me get back on the field. I was named the starting tailback on offense and I was used occasionally to return kickoffs.

Mr. "Ironman"

Along the way, I had to make a tough decision concerning wrestling. To remain in my weight class meant constant dieting, but to get stronger and tougher on the football field I needed to put on a few extra pounds. Well, my love for food outweighed my love for wrestling and I gave up the sport. Now it was just football and running track.

At LaGrange High one of the great traditions is the "Ironman" competition that has been an annual event for as long as anyone can remember. It involved earning scores in a number of physical activities including the bench press, box jumps, 40-yard dash, half-mile run, and points for the most workouts.

My main rival was a student named Fred. He was much stronger than I was and a defensive middle-linebacker on the football squad. It was a big boost to my ego when I beat him for the title—mainly because of my overall abilities. I won the honor in both my junior and senior years.

SHATTERED DREAMS

So here I was, mister "Ironman," a senior starter for the Grangers, being looked at by college scouts, and relishing in the feeling I was something special.

Then came my emotional outburst after being scolded because I was late for practice. Like a mental YouTube video, I can still see myself throwing my helmet down and walking off the field.

In an instant, my whole world collapsed.

When the college athletic scholarships were announced, my name was never mentioned.

Inside, I was devastated, saying to myself, "What a waste of time all of this has been. Tyrone, you are a loser. You'll never play football again."

My dreams were shattered. Here I was, at the age of eighteen, feeling like I had reached the end of the road.

Where would I turn? What would my future hold?

Chapter 2

Life Beyond Church's Chicken

The summer of 1990 was blistering hot—and I was completely frustrated. I had to choke back the tears when so many of those in my high school graduating class were bragging about the colleges they would be attending. It was especially painful to know that an athletic scholarship would likely have been mine if I had not been so stubborn and quit the football team.

To pocket a little spending money, I found a job at Church's Chicken on New Franklin Road. It was quite a distance from our house, but my grandad was a mechanic who was very good at fixing up used cars and he gave me an old blue Buick Skylark. You should have seen it! It was really a mix-match—with a front fender from a junkyard car in another color.

Freebies from the Fryer

At Church's, when I worked there, all the employees took turns cooking chicken. I didn't mind this assignment since it gave me a chance to sample the freshest and best food.

When my time rolled around, the store manager would tell me how many pans of chicken he needed cut for the "now shift" and for later. Then I'd put on a thick coat, a pair of gloves, and head for the ice-cold walk-in freezer.

The chickens were trucked in whole, and after turning on the electric saw, I'd take a wing and thigh in my right hand, the same in my left hand and push the chicken through the blade to cut it in half. Next, I'd saw off the smaller pieces and put the legs, wings, thighs, and breasts in separate containers.

Messy work, but part of the job.

It felt like a day at the beach to get out of that

freezer and bring the pans to the kitchen and plop the chicken into the deep fryer. Then came my favorite part. When business was slow, I'd grab a chicken breast, hide behind a corner wall, and sample my cooking.

Of course, tasty as they were, those freebies caused me to put on a few extra pounds!

My buddies headed off for college in September, but I didn't have enough money to enroll and my prospects looked rather dim. So I stayed behind in LaGrange, serving chicken into the fall and early winter.

I soon found out that my old car didn't have a heater—but there was an opening near the accelerator pedal that let some of the heat from the engine escape into the passenger section. Better than nothing!

FINDING A WAY

I had a wonderful teacher at LaGrange High named Mrs. Heard, who had graduated from a small college in Georgia called Fort Valley State—about an hour and a half from where we lived. She not only bragged about the school, but did everything possible to encourage students to enroll there.

It was Mrs. Heard who worked with me in preparation for passing the entrance exam—and doing the paperwork necessary to obtain a need-based Pell grant and a student loan.

The college was operating on the quarter system at that time, and the earliest I would be able to enroll was in January, 1991.

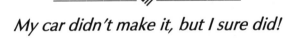

My car didn't make it, but I sure did!

WOULD THEY ACCEPT A "WALK ON"?

Fort Valley opened a whole new world for me. It's an historically black college with a rich history that has now gained university status. I loved the student life and felt at home there from the beginning.

When springtime finally came around, I mustered up enough courage to find the track coach and asked if I could be a "walk on" and try out for the squad.

Not only was I warmly received, but after a few workouts, he told me, "Tyrone, I usually don't do this just before track season, but I want to give you a partial athletic scholarship if you will join the team right now."

Under my breath I was shouting, "Hallelujah!"

———————— •» ————————

Immediately, they had me running the 100 and 200 meter sprints, the quarter mile, plus I was on the 4x4 relay team.

Evidently, because of my speed, word spread to other athletic departments, and I was invited to try out for football. To my amazement, they offered me another scholarship which would kick in that fall. That was good news.

While my parents weren't big sports fans, I knew their prayers for me to have a college education were being answered.

CHANGING DIRECTIONS

This was my second chance at football and I wasn't

about to blow it!

My first year playing for the "Wildcats," they had me all over the field. I caught kickoffs and punts, and because I was a running back in high school they placed me on the offensive side of the ball as a tailback.

I was really impressed with the head coach, Doug Porter, who later became a College Football Hall of Fame Coach.

I listened to every word he said and followed his orders without question.

It wasn't long, however, until one of the defensive coaches, Dean Brown, came over to me and said, "Tyrone, we've made the decision to switch you from offense. We want you to be a defensive back." Then he added, "I like your quick feet and the way you can change directions. Plus, you're really strong for your size."

Who was I to argue with his decision? After all, coach Brown had played in the NFL for both the Cleveland Browns and the Miami Dolphins. I'll never forget the day he handed me a pair of thigh pads, and commented, "These are the ones I wore when I was in the pros. I want you to have them."

They became a prized possession.

My position was right cornerback—and I held it for my entire college career. I don't know how I did it, but I was a starter in 41 of the 42 games we played while I was at Fort Valley.

We were members of the Southern Intercollegiate Conference and played an NCAA Division II schedule against teams including, Valdosta State, North Alabama, Tuskegee, Jacksonville State, and Alabama A&M.

THE LEGACY

Half way through my junior year, a few people began whispering that I might have a chance to play in the pros. Of course, being a late bloomer, I brushed that notion aside. After all, at 5'9", I thought I was too short to be considered as a player to go up against those tall receivers in the NFL.

Plus, I was playing for a small school. Would they really take note of me?

My fellow teammates told me not to worry about the size of our college or the level of competition we played. "If you're good, they are certainly going to find you."

I learned the stories of Fort Valley players who had gone before me—and made it to the pros. They included:

- Rayfield Wright, a 1967 seventh-round draft pick who played offensive tackle for the Dallas Cowboys and became a member of the Pro Football Hall of Fame.

- Eddie Anderson, a 1986 sixth-round pick who played safety for the Seattle Seahawks and the Oakland Raiders.

- Greg Lloyd, a 1987 sixth-round pick who became an outstanding linebacker for the Pittsburgh Steelers.

The pros? Was it really possible?
As a kid I was a huge fan of the Dallas Cowboys

and even imagined myself suiting up in silver and blue. My favorite player was running back Tony Dorsett—so much so that I took a marker and wrote a big "33" on the back of one of my T-shirts.

My mom was not impressed. "Son, don't do that again. We can't afford to mess up good clothes like that."

On Track

Back on campus, members of the team would point out scouts hovering around the sidelines, "I think they're looking at you, Tyrone," they would joke.

Meanwhile, I kept my eyes focused on making every practice count and being sure I was prepared for those important Saturday games.

I was also serious about my track and field events—and it really paid off.

———— ·»> ————

My sophomore, junior, and senior years I qualified for national NCAA Division II competition.

As a junior, the 1994 nationals were held at a university in Abilene, Texas, and it was my very first ride on an airplane. I was a white-knuckle passenger on that Delta flight from Atlanta to Dallas. And on the second leg of the journey I was a basket case. It was a small prop plane into Abilene and it was vibrating so violently that I thought the nuts and bolts would come loose!

I made it to the semifinals in the 200-meter.

My senior year, I was more determined than ever. Nationals were held in Raleigh, North Carolina, and I gave every race my all. The end result was that I came in fifth in the 100-meter run and second in the 200-meter event.

Of course, I was quite disappointed in not taking first place, but my coach encouraged me, saying, "What are you worrying about? There's only one person in the nation that is faster than you in the 200 in our division. Your record is something to be proud of."

They Were Watching

My final year of football at Fort Valley was unreal. I had made a few national lists of "players to watch," as defensive backs.

---◈---

The pros were showing up every week—at our games, during our practice sessions, and even requesting films of our games.

I later found out that during my college years the scouts went all the way back to my high school coach to talk with him. I'm sure he was honest about what happened during my final year at LaGrange High —and that I had learned a valuable lesson from the experience.

Scouting has become so sophisticated and detailed that if a player has talent they are going to know about it. Even when you are in your freshman or sophomore years, when they are looking at older players, they'll also hear about you and start making notes.

During warm-ups I would spot the scouts standing along the sidelines talking with the coaches. They were hard to ignore dressed in their Cleveland Browns or Minnesota Vikings hats or shirts.

When they walked over to where the corners and safeties were practicing, I knew they were looking at me. So I made sure I always showed up on time and gave it everything I had.

During part of that final season, coach Brown had another assignment over in Macon, Georgia, so if he was going to be a little late for practice, he would ask me and some of the other seniors to run drills for our group.

I didn't mind a bit since it hopefully gave the scouts a chance to observe our leadership skills.

BOWL TIME

One of my biggest thrills was being the first player in the history of Fort Valley to be invited to play in the annual Blue-Gray game, in Montgomery, Alabama, on Christmas Day, 1994.

This is where outstanding seniors from northern

colleges and universities (Blues) play against those from the south (Grays). Even though the northerners won, 38-27, it was a tremendous opportunity for those from the NFL to see me in action.

An even greater honor came my way a few weeks later when I was asked to play in the prestigious Senior Bowl in Mobile, Alabama.

This event had a star-studded roster that included quarterbacks Steve McNair, Kerry Collins, and Derrick Brooks (the Florida State linebacker who later won a Super Bowl with Tampa Bay).

If there was ever an opportunity to make a name for yourself, this was it.

Head coaches and scouts from virtually every NFL team descended on the site. Our coach for the game was Ted Marchibroda of the Indianapolis Colts.

The Senior Bowl gave me the platform to show that I was capable of playing at the highest level. However, I have to admit that on the first day of practice I was more than a little star-struck to see players from major universities like Florida and Texas whom I had admired and watched on televison.

Fortunately, when I started going against those players in practice, I found out that I was just as strong and fast as they were.

Not only did I hold my own, I was making plays, breaking up passes, and snagging interceptions.

In Mobile, even during the one-on-one drills with receivers, I was on my game.

The head coaches who were watching would dictate who they wanted to see in the number one spot—and the game coaches would comply. Before the draft, they want to see how you're going to do against a receiver who is supposedly a first round pick. It gives them a chance to compare apples with apples.

So I was penciled in to run with the first team defense. I could tell by the way the coaches interacted with me that there was plenty of interest.

My friends back home were really surprised when football analyst Mel Kiper said on ESPN, "He looks like a kid out of UCLA."

Could it Be?

To me, the fact that our south team won 14-7 was besides the point. I had been given a golden opportunity and the good Lord helped me make the most of it.

This was January, and the 1995 NFL draft was just three months away. Was it possible? Could it be that one more player from Fort Valley State could make it to the big time?

I thought, "If Rayfield Wright was picked in the seventh round, maybe, just maybe there would be a spot for me."

Chapter 3

A Prayer that Came True

During the early months of 1995, I felt like I was riding a Ferris wheel and couldn't quite figure out if it was going up or down.

In one ear I was hearing, "Tyrone, you're a lock for the NFL draft. No doubt about it."

In the other ear, I could hear the advice my parents had given me for years: "Son, if you are going to play sports, make sure you get a degree. You always need something to fall back on in case things don't turn out the way you think they will."

This was my final year at Fort Valley and I knew what I had learned as a business major would help me the rest of my life.

Yet, I can't describe the excitement I felt at the very thought of playing ball on national television and earning more money than my mental calculator could count.

The Combine

In February I received an invitation to travel to Indianapolis for the NFL Combine. This is where hundreds of prospective pro players are brought to one location where they go through medical examinations and participate in a variety of psychological and physical tests. In addition, there are formal and informal interviews with top executives, coaches, and scouts from all 32 NFL teams. It's been called "The ultimate four-day job interview" for the top college football players eligible for the upcoming NFL draft.

They clocked and scored me in everything from the 40-yard dash to the bench press, vertical jump, broad jump, 3-cone drill, 20-yard shuttle, and 60-yard shuttle.

I thought I survived the rigorous ordeal, but how do you really know when you are being compared with so many other talented athletes?

As my anxiety rose, I kept thinking of the words of Jesus: "If you have faith as a mustard seed, you will say to this mountain, 'Move from here to there,' and it will move; and nothing will be impossible for you."

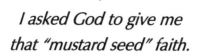

*I asked God to give me
that "mustard seed" faith.*

WOULD I NEED AN AGENT?

In preparation for what *might* be happening in my future, I was receiving all kinds of advice—some solicited and some not. More than once, people told me, "You'd better get a good sports agent. Don't try to step into the big time all by yourself."

In fact, I had been receiving phone calls and letters from a large number of agents. Most of them, however, were rather impersonal—just bragging about the players they represented and their track record of success. Some even sent what I called "runners," to shake my hand and give me a sales pitch. These were not the top executives in the firm, but reps who were fishing to see how many potential athletes they could bait and reel in.

I finally decided to go with Hadley Englehard of Enter-Sports Management with offices located in Atlanta and around the country. Why him? Because he personally came to see me and we just "clicked."

While he wasn't the most well-known agent, he handled people such as Dorsey Levens, a Pro-Bowl running back for the Green Bay Packers.

Quickly, I learned that professional athletes in this generation are more talented than ever before. They also make more money, have greater opportunities, face more pressures, and are subjected to higher demands—and are perhaps more vulnerable—than almost any other public figure. If I was going to be fortunate enough to enter this arena, I needed someone to handle contract negotiations, possible product endorsements, and marketing opportunities. And I hoped I would need top-notch financial and tax planning.

It was certainly a lot to consider.

Something in the Air

I began ticking off the days until April 22, 1995. That was the start of the NFL draft which was scheduled to be held at the Radio City Music Hall in New York City.

In those years, only the top ten potential first round pick were invited to be there in person. The rest of the athletes would be watching the announcements on national television.

The so-called experts had me being selected anywhere from the 16th pick in the first round all the way to the end—seven rounds and more than 250 athletes later.

Of course, I could miss the draft altogether.

However, I felt something good was in the air when ESPN sent a television field crew to interview me at our home in LaGrange and filmed my workouts on campus at Fort Valley. I was getting the "major college player" treatment.

Frankie's was Buzzing!

By April there was no avoiding the topic. My friends wanted to know, "Where's the draft party?"

My agent, and a number of other people booked Frankie's restaurant in Atlanta for what they hoped would be a big celebration. I even splurged and had a new suit made—the first time I ever had a custom-tailored suit in my life.

Everyone in my extended family showed up—aunts, uncles, and cousins I hadn't seen for years. What a scene it was: local sports broadcasters, the Atlanta Falcons cheerleaders, and people I didn't even know. Also present was Billy "White Shoes" Johnson, a colorful kick returner who had played for the Houston Oilers and the Atlanta Falcons in the 70s and 80s.

Because of a number of phone calls I had received, it looked promising that I was going to be picked in the first round by the Detroit Lions. They had shown exceptional interest in me.

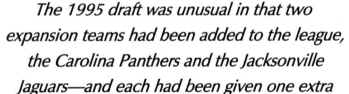

The 1995 draft was unusual in that two expansion teams had been added to the league, the Carolina Panthers and the Jacksonville Jaguars—and each had been given one extra pick during the first and second rounds.

Frankie's was buzzing by the time the draft began. First to be named was Ki-Jana Carter, a powerful running back from Penn State who was selected by the Cincinnati Bengals. In the third and fifth spots were quarterbacks Steve McNair and Kerry Collins, who went to Houston and Carolina respectively. Defensive end, Warren Sapp was chosen by Tampa Bay at number 12.

When Detroit was on the clock with the 20th pick, I just knew my name was about to be called, and I held my breath. Then the announcement came: "The Detroit Lions have selected Luther Elliss, a defensive tackle from Utah."

My heart sank. Where would that leave me? Would I even go in the first round—or was it going to be a long night?

"Get in Here!"

Taking a break, I walked outside where fans wanted to take a few pictures and have me sign more autographs. No problem. I needed a little diversion from the disappointment of not hearing my name called.

Then, all of a sudden, I heard the voice of my agent, Hadley Englehard. "Tyrone," he yelled, "get in here. You've got an important call!"

I followed him to the back of the kitchen and picked up the phone. "Is this Tyrone Poole?" asked the voice on the other end.

"Yes, sir," I responded crisply.

"This is Bill Polian, general manager of the Carolina Panthers. We are going to take you as our next selection."

About the same time I heard a loud commotion in the restaurant. Toy horns were blowing like it was New Year's Eve. People were yelling loud enough to raise the roof!

Evidently, on television, they were watching NFL Commissioner, Paul Tagliabue as he announced, "For the 22nd selection, the Carolina Panthers have chosen Tyrone Poole of Fort Valley State College."

Through the noise, Polian asked me, "How do you feel about being a Carolina Panther?"

As my mind was racing, I thought, "What kind of question is that?" Being on the roster of an NFL team was all I ever dreamed of.

Trying to remain as calm and professional as possible, I answered, "I would love to be with Carolina."

At that moment it felt as though my heart was bursting out of my chest.

Next on the line was Dom Capers, the first head coach of the Panthers who was hired from the Pittsburgh Steelers. He welcomed me to the team and told me how excited they were to have me. Wow! Was this really happening?

A Prayer that Came True

I took a deep breath and walked out into Frankie's restaurant and the room erupted in cheers. My parents rushed over to my side and my mom was in tears. Dad tried to stay strong, but he too was overcome with emotion.

I really didn't want to break down and start crying in front of everybody so I slipped into the restroom for a moment and shed a few tears on my own before composing myself. When I returned there were a rash of calls from reporters, especially those from Carolina requesting interviews.

———— ❧ ————

There were plenty of first's for me that night. I was the first defensive cornerback to be drafted that year—and I was the first Fort Valley player ever to be drafted in the first round of the NFL.

When the cheers subsided and my friends made

their way home, it was just the three of us—me, my mom and dad.

We found a place alone to talk about the changes that would soon be taking place. I had always wanted a better life for them, and it was about to happen.

My mind flashed back to a night when I was just a youngster. It is still fresh in my memory. Mom was on her knees in the corner of the room praying, "Lord, I believe You have a calling on Tyrone's life and You will bless him abundantly. He will be the Moses of our family. We won't have to live like this forever."

Her prayers were coming true.

Chapter 4

"This is What You Are Playing For"

Talk about nervous! You should have been in my shoes the first day I walked into the Carolina Panthers mini-camp at Winthrop College in Rock Hill, South Carolina.

This was the big time! When the introductions were being made, even though I was a first-round draft choice, I instantly knew the competition was going to be stiff.

This was the inaugural season for the Panthers and everything was new. I was immediately impressed with my position coach, George Catavolos, who had come from the Indianapolis Colts, and defensive coordinator, Vic Fangio, hired from the New Orleans Saints. I also felt good that head coach, Dom Capers had focused on my side of the ball. During his three years as defensive coordinator at Pittsburgh, the Steelers defense surrendered the fewest points in the NFL.

Talent was everywhere. I met the other first-round draft picks, quarterback Kerry Collins, tackle Brock Brockermeyer, plus Frank Reich, a seasoned quarterback who came to Carolina from the Buffalo Bills in the expansion draft.

Winning the Lottery!

Everything seemed to be happening at lightning speed. My agent had negotiated what to me seemed like a mind-boggling contract.

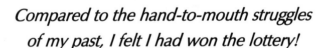

Compared to the hand-to-mouth struggles of my past, I felt I had won the lottery!

One thing I knew for sure, I wasn't going to be foolish with my money. My agent had spent hours talking with me about how short a professional football career can be—the NFL Players Association says the average player is in the league only 3.3 years.

Unfortunately, many squander their instant wealth

like there is no tomorrow. They splurge on mansions, luxury cars, fly to Las Vegas at the drop of a hat, and choose a lifestyle of wine, women, and song. Then one day they wake up and find themselves broke!

My first purchases as a pro were a $200,000 home in Charlotte and a Jeep Cherokee. More important, however, I was able to see my mom's prayers come true as I bought my parents a much better house back in LaGrange, Georgia. They loved it—especially my father, who immediately sought out a spot to grow his flowers and vegetables.

All through my life I heard the stories of my mother's dad who, even though he didn't have much to spare, would give his last dollar to a person who was in need. He had the reputation of being a generous man, and I believe that through him a generational blessing had fallen on me.

———— ❥ ————

Now it was my time to give.

A Special Day

Since the new Panther stadium was still under

construction in downtown Charlotte, we played our inaugural season in what is called "Death Valley," at Clemson University in South Carolina.

The predictions by sports analysts around the country were that we would win no more than one or two games. However, coach Capers drilled his style of play into us: "I want you to out-smart and out-play every opponent," he would drum into us.

———————— » ————————

Capers believed the "cerebral" or mental side of football was every bit as important as size and strength.

After the first five games of the 1995 season, I was beginning to think the analysts were right. We had five losses and no wins—and were about to play some of our toughest opponents.

On October 15, the New York Jets came to Clemson. It was a special day for me in more ways than one. At a critical point in the game their quarterback, Bubby Brister, threw a pass and I had my first NFL interception.

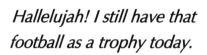

Hallelujah! I still have that football as a trophy today.

We beat the Jets 26-15 for our first victory. During the next two weeks we surprised the football world with wins over the New Orleans Saints (20-3) and an overtime victory against the New England Patriots (20-17).

FACING THE CHAMPS

Our winning streak would surely come to an abrupt halt the next week when we flew out to San Francisco to take on the 49ers at 3Com Park. They had won the Super Bowl earlier that same year and I was really pumped up.

I can close my eyes right now and visualize some of the plays of that game on November 5, 1995. Once, when I was guarding the All-Pro Jerry Rice, he caught an end route and broke it back to the sidelines at about our 15-yard line. He had experience, but I had youth and I kept telling myself, "Tyrone, you are faster than he is."

On that play, I was able to catch up with Rice just as he was about to cross the goal line. I reached out and punched the ball out of his arm and it went through the back of the end zone—which is a touchback. No score for Frisco!

Later in the game, receiver John Taylor caught a ball as he was going across the middle of the field. So I did what I was taught: go for the ball and don't quit until you hear the whistle.

He was carrying the football in his right arm, so when I caught up with him, I wrapped my left arm around his waist. Then I took my right hand and grabbed the pigskin, which caused a fumble. Again, he was about to score, but Sam Mills fell on the ball for us on the 2-yard line.

When it was over, the Panthers had won its fourth game in a row, 13-7. On the flight home I was all smiles, knowing what I had contributed that day. More impressive, it was the first time in league history that an expansion team had defeated the defending Super Bowl champion.

Moving On

That first year we wound up with a 7-9 record

(most wins ever by an expansion team). Then, when the awards were being handed out, I was amazed to be named with Deion Sanders, Brett Favre, and Emmit Smith on the All-Madden NFL team. Plus I was on several All-Rookie rosters.

The following season, 1996, Capers led the team to a record of 12–4 and a division title. We advanced to the NFC Conference Championship, but fell to the Green Bay Packers 30–13, who went on to win the Super Bowl. In that second season with the Panthers I was fortunate enough to have 80 tackles—and 65 were solo.

After three years with Carolina, Bill Polian, who had left the Panthers to become the general manger of the Indianapolis Colts, worked behind the scenes to have me traded to his team.

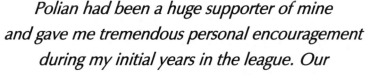

Polian had been a huge supporter of mine and gave me tremendous personal encouragement during my initial years in the league. Our friendship continues to this day.

Now I was on the same team with a rookie quarterback for the 1998 season—Peyton Manning.

Perhaps you have heard of him! In case you have forgotten, during his first year the Colts had a record of 3 wins and 13 losses.

My three years as a starter with Indianapolis were rewarding—amassing a total of 120 tackles. At the same time I was earning a high salary—and those who know football understand that it is a business. As a result, I became a salary cap casualty and was released in 2001 before signing with the Denver Broncos. I loved playing for Mike Shanahan.

During 2002 I had some exciting games, including eight solo tackles against both Oakland and Kansas City.

THE BIG GAME

I finished my contract with the Broncos, became a free agent, and signed with the New England Patriots. What fun! I was one of four defensive players to start all 19 games in the regular and post-season contests.

Against the New York Giants I enjoyed picking off my old Carolina teammate, Kerry Collins on the first play of the game. Then I stripped Tiki Barber of the ball, resulting in Matt Chatham's 38-yard return for the initial score. And I certainly took great satisfaction in intercepting Peyton Manning in the third quarter of our game with the Colts that year.

What a season! Our record for 2003 was 14-2. Then after bulldozing our way through the playoffs, we made it to Super Bowl 38 against—who would have guessed it—the Carolina Panthers.

My jersey number was 38, and I felt the Lord may have had something special for me that February 1, 2004, at Reliant Stadium in Houston, Texas.

"Which Ring Do You Want?"

The night before the game, coach Bill Belichick, wearing a tan suit, stood before our team and focused our minds on what was about to happen. "Men," he began, "there is no other game after tomorrow. It is the Super Bowl."

Then he pulled two rings out of his pocket. One had been presented to him when the Patriots won Super Bowl 36, just two years earlier.

The second ring was one they give to members of

the losing team. Then he finished by asking, "Which ring do you want?" As he held up the champion's ring, he motivated us all with these words: "This is what you are playing for tomorrow."

The enormity of the situation hit home. This was our chance to have more than a memory— it would be a lasting legacy we would leave for our children, and their children.

As game time approached, during warm-ups I had an opportunity to connect with several of my former teammates who were still with Carolina. Jerry Richardson, the club owner, was especially kind to me during our brief conversation.

Then it was down to business. In a surprisingly close high-scoring game, the Patriots came out victorious, 32-29.

I had my ring—and I wasn't about to let it go!

Was this the End?

Since the 2003 season was so rewarding, I was

chomping at the bit to hit the field in 2004. Our team was intact and we felt the Patriots would be stronger than ever.

During our third game, after we had defeated the Indianapolis Colts and the Arizona Cardinals, we traveled to Buffalo to take on the Bills.

On one particular play I was covering Lee Evans, a rookie receiver. We were both running side by side and I jumped to make a play on the ball. But when I came down I twisted my right knee and knew immediately I had done some serious damage.

I was helped off the field and when the team doctor examined my leg he said, "I think you need to have an MRI."

The results revealed that I had torn my meniscus. This is the cartilage that helps cushion the tibula and fibula bones of the lower leg.

Then I was told, "The place of the tear will not grow back so you will need an operation to cut it out. But I'm sure they will save as much as possible."

To make matters worse, one of the Patriot trainers let me know, "Tyrone, you may not be able to jump and do all the things you've done in the past." Then he told me of other players who had suffered similar injuries which ended their careers.

One twenty-two year old who had the same injury showed me the big knot that sits on the outside of his knee. Was that going to be me?

Immediately, the Patriots placed me on the injury list and the trainers began working on my leg.

Believe me when I tell you that it was more than frustrating to be sidelined on what promised to be another championship season.

Chapter 5

The Turn-Around

I have never claimed to be a saint. In fact during my early years in the NFL, as a single guy, I did my share of running around.

Let's face it. Coming into the league you suddenly find yourself in the spotlight of glamor, money, and fame. It's tempting to start believing the hype written about you—and this happened to me.

In Charlotte, one of my endorsement contracts was with Reebok and Kerry Collins was with Nike. We used to tease each other about our shoes, but I admit it was an ego boost to drive through the city and see my image emblazoned on those Reebok billboards.

I didn't have to look for a date. More than once, when a young lady found out I was playing for the

Panthers, she'd hand me her phone number.

Because of the first-class treatment I received, I began to think "It's all about me."

SOMEONE SPECIAL

One night in 1997, during my third season with Carolina, my friend Herman Williams and I were at T.G.I. Friday's on Independence Boulevard on the east side of town.

After getting a bite to eat we were hanging out in the parking lot when, suddenly, out of the door of the restaurant walked two very sharp ladies. "Herman," I suggested, "why don't you work your charm and see if you can strike up a conversation with them?"

He did, and we were bold enough to ask them a few questions and joke around for a bit. One of the young women was named Jennifer.

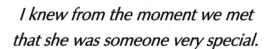

I knew from the moment we met that she was someone very special.

I was so impressed that I was brave enough to ask

if I could get in touch with her again. Which I did.

This young lady was far different than anyone I had ever dated. She was almost as tall as me, very athletic, highly motivated, and independent. The whole package!

Jennifer was raised in a strong home and her mom was one of those shouting Pentecostal women who really let loose in church. At times her enthusiasm for the Lord embarrassed Jennifer and her brother, who also attended. But they loved her dearly.

We continued getting to know each other and after a year or so, Jennifer and I began talking about the prospect of marriage. However, there were aspects of my personality and behavior that evidently bothered her. It seemed that conflicts of one kind or another were always rising to the surface.

Was it Over?

In the spring of 2000, after another season with the Indianapolis Colts, Jennifer and I had a major disagreement. It escalated to the point that I thought our relationship was totally over.

"We can't go on this way," she told me.

Afraid of losing Jennifer, I got alone and took a

long, hard, introspective look at myself—and didn't like what I saw. I came to the conclusion, "This is not how I should be acting."

I inherited many traits from my dad, a rather quiet individual who avoided confrontations or arguments, although he may have had strong feelings.

Jennifer was emotional and I wasn't.

Even though I was a professional athlete, I was quite immature in many ways and felt the sun was always shining brightly on me.

As a young adult, I had become used to making my own decisions. There was no one around to advise, "Tyrone, this is wrong." I was setting my own standards and they certainly weren't always the highest or the best. It was all about what "I" wanted, and what "I" decided.

"Dear God!"

That day, however, I began to think that if our wedding was really going to take place in a few short months, I had better make some changes in a hurry. I knew that marriage was supposed to involve mutual respect between a man and a woman who truly loved each other. Into my mind popped a verse from the Bible I had heard many times in church: "[How] can two walk together, unless they are agreed?" (Amos 3:3).

At that moment, I fell on my knees and began talking to the Lord: "Dear God," I cried out, "I don't want to be like this any more. Change me. Give me peace. Forgive me for being so self-centered. Help me to be the person You want me to be."

This was not a short, glib prayer. I stayed before the Lord and poured out my heart and made a commitment to God unlike any I had ever prayed before.

In a marriage between Jennifer and myself, I didn't want to be a problem, but a solution.

A Dramatic Transformation

Looking back on my life, I had attended church for as long as I could remember, being baptized at the age of seven. In the pros, every team has a chaplain and there is always a voluntary Sunday morning service before the games. I was there. And during our dating years, Jennifer and I attended church.

Spiritually, however, God seemed to be just a convenient part of my life—not the center and the absolute core of who I was and the ultimate standard of how I was living.

Now it was time for a dramatic transformation. The world would no longer revolve around my own needs, wants, and desires. I realized that two people coming together with different views could never be happy unless there was a determined effort to seek unity instead of discord, harmony instead of hostility.

I was the one who needed to change, and with God's help, I did.

Feeding a Starving Spirit

When I rededicated my life to the Lord, my physical man didn't become reborn, but my spiritual man sure did. To explain it as simply as possible, I like to put it this way: if you come to God and you are baldheaded, repentance doesn't suddenly give you hair. However, you do have a re-created spirit.

I was at a point in my life where my "flesh" had been well-fed because of what I watched, listened to, and acted out—but my spirit was starving. As a result,

I had been making wrong decisions and it was damaging my personal relationships.

My mom started sending me VHS tapes with messages of godly men such as Fredrick Price, Bill Winston, and I.V. Hilliard. Slowly but surely my faith was increasing and my daily life was being made new.

I realized that I had not become a professional athlete overnight—there was a growing, learning, and maturing process involved. Now the same thing was happening in my heart, mind and soul.

Even more important, I was now on the right track and ready to face the future.

Jennifer and I were married on June 24, 2000, and God has blessed us with a wonderful life and three loving children, Nakai, Tyra, and Tyson.

Something Much Bigger than Football

Returning to the Indianapolis Colts for the 2000 season, then on to Denver and finally New England, I may have been the same Tyrone Poole on the field, but inside I was a brand new man—and those around me knew it.

On January 28, 2004, a few days before we were to play Carolina in Super Bowl 38, *USA Today* published a major story under the headline, "Poole's Faith Carries Him to Banner Season."

Sports writer Pete O'Brien got it right when he observed, "Tyrone Poole spends hour after hour studying his playbook. But he is consumed by The Book."

In the interview I explained that God came first, my family second, and football third—and how that order of priorities had never steered me wrong.

When the writer asked me how I handled the big receivers in the league, I used David and Goliath as an example. And he quoted my answer word for word: "In my Bible it tells me that 'greater is he that is in me than he that is in the world,' so I play with that mentality which allows me to overcome and conquer certain circumstances that other people figure I shouldn't be able to do."

The article concluded, "Poole's stellar play in the postseason is in part because he doesn't feel the pressure many others do because he knows there is something much bigger than football."

THE POWER OF CONFESSION

I wore my Super Bowl ring with pride, but had no

idea that my football career would come crashing down the next fall in that early season game between the Patriots and the Buffalo Bills.

"Ouch, that really hurts," I moaned to myself as I hit the turf and twisted my right knee after trying to make a play against receiver Lee Evans.

It was my worst fear. I had torn my meniscus and would be out for the season. However, when a trainer told me, "That knee will probably never be the same again," I totally ignored his remark. Why? Because I believed the words of the Bible: "Death and life are in the power of the tongue" (Proverbs 18:21) and I knew that what you say is what you get!

So immediately, I began confessing strength and success instead of failure and defeat. "You're going to come back from this, stronger than ever, "I told myself.

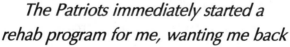

The Patriots immediately started a rehab program for me, wanting me back on the field as soon as possible.

Just five weeks after my injury, the Patriots were hosting the Cincinnati Bengals, December 12, 2004, and I convinced the coaching staff I was ready to get back on the field.

They let me play, but during the game my knee was still tender and I suffered another injury. So I was placed on Injured Reserve and they allowed me to return to our home in Atlanta to work with an outstanding sports-injury specialist I knew there.

All I could do was watch the Patriots on television as they finished their regular season with another 14-2 record.

During every play, I was thinking, "I really need to be in there."

"Keep Going"

One morning, not long after I had started my come-back program, I was sitting in a chair we have in our bedroom and began to cry.

Jennifer came in and wanted to know, "What's wrong?"

I was not crying out of sadness, but out of anger. I had just come from our downstairs weight room and was not even able to lift five pounds with my right leg.

Please understand, I was an athlete who was used

to doing leg extensions with 70 to 90 pounds, one leg at a time.

When I couldn't lift five pounds, you can imagine my frustration and disappointment.

Jennifer tried her best to give me faith and encouragement. "Keep going," she said, "You'll be okay."

The next day, I went downstairs, put the weights on again, and even though it was painful, with grit and determination I added five more pounds. I was still upset being only able to lift ten pounds.

Day after day, week after week, I kept making strides—even though at times it was sheer agony. I finally reached the point where I could do a 70-pound right leg extension.

ANOTHER SETBACK

Through the favor of God and being surrounded by positive people, I felt I was ready to go back to New England and show them my progress.

The playoffs were coming up and I was determined to get back to New England as fast as humanly possible. Every player in the NFL worries, "If I turn up injured, I will get released." I was no exception.

In my case, I had to show them I was back to my old self and ready to return for the next season—or there might not be another contract.

A Skeptical Staff

Just before the first playoff game against Indianapolis, I flew to New England and announced, "I'm ready."

The staff was skeptical, so the trainers put me to the test and had me perform a series of exercises. One of the strength coaches had a device that measured the ratio of speed to strength. He first put a cord to the knee of my non-injured leg to get a baseline figure to compare with my right leg.

It registered in the 90s on that first test. Then he said, "Let's hook this up to your right leg." In one ear I was hearing the words, "Okay, Tyrone, are you ready for this?"

I knew if I did anything less than 90, they'd report it to the head coach and my days as a Patriot might be over.

But the voice in my other ear was encouraging and coaxing me, "You are ready. Block everything else out. Do what you have to do." With the weights in my hand, I stood on my right leg without my left foot even touching the floor and performed a single-leg squat on the right side of my body. When I came up, I looked at the meter and it registered the same number as my left leg.

Praise God!

The Final Whistle

I was back with the team as we posted wins against Indianapolis and Pittsburgh in the playoffs.

On February 6, 2005, at Alltel Stadium in Jacksonville, Florida, the Patriots faced the Philadelphia Eagles in Super Bowl 39.

It was a close contest with New England coming out on top, 24-21.

When the final whistle blew and the celebrating began, some of the players gathered around me and exclaimed, "Tyrone, you are a two-time Super Bowl champion."

Believe me, I certainly knew who deserved all the thanks.

Chapter 6

Be a Thoroughbred, not a Donkey

Someone recently asked me, "What do you remember about your college coach?"

Doug Porter, who led our team at Fort Valley State the entire time I was there, had a unique way of mixing motivation with humor to get his point across. He loved to smile, but was deadly serious about winning football games.

One day at a player's meeting he told us: "I want you to be thoroughbreds, not donkeys."

Then he pointed out the difference between the two. Thoroughbreds are known for their agility, speed, and spirit. They're born to run. Donkey's, however, may pull a load one day, then the next, when you are ready for them to work, they will sit down. Stubborn by nature, it is extremely difficult to get them to change their ways.

Later I learned that when a group of thoroughbred horses face attack from an outside enemy, they form a circle facing each other, then kick out at the attackers using their strongest muscle—their hind legs? On the other hand their ornery relatives, donkeys, do just the opposite. They circle up, facing the enemy, and use their hind legs to kick each other. Not so smart!

Coach Porter kept drilling the phrase into us: "We need more thoroughbreds and fewer donkeys."

THE PARALLEL WITH BUSINESS

Over a period of 14 seasons in the NFL, I ran up and down the field with the best of the best. After three years with the Patriots I signed with the Oakland Raiders in 2006 and finished my professional career with the Tennessee Titans in 2008.

Along the way, growing up, in high school, college

and the pros, I discovered many important principles that not only apply to the sport of football, but to this journey called life. They have guided my past, keep me on track in the present, and I know they will steer my future.

Recently, I was speaking to a group of business professionals about the parallels between the corporate world and athletics. Much of the routine is exactly the same.

For example, an executive has to spend hours in preparation, meet with the staff on Monday morning, decide on objectives for the week, go over the numbers and statistics, know the competition, adjust to circumstances, and be ready to lead.

This is really not too different from a typical week in the NFL:

- Monday—Hit the weight room with the trainers. Check out any injuries. Review the game film with the coaches, Listen to the assessment of the head coach on what went right, what went wrong, and how to improve.
- Tuesday—Usually the day off to take care of personal business.
- Wednesday—Tough day. Team meetings to

study film of opponent and devise the game plan. Hit the weights. Team practice. Study the play book.
- Thursday—Usually the same as Wednesday but no lifting. Study play book.
- Friday—Morning weigh-in (either be on target or get fined!) Hit the weights. No-pad team workout. Study play book.
- Saturday—Pump iron and have team walk-through of game plan. Fly to destination or check in team hotel at home. Have dinner with the players. Chapel. Study play book.
- Sunday—Game day.

Professional football is a business—not much different than the basics of running a McDonald's franchise or a clothing store. Those who treat it as a sport or a hobby soon find themselves out of the league.

Every successful enterprise involves working with men and women who come from a variety of cultures and backgrounds—whether they are your associates, clients, or customers. If you can't relate to others, you'll soon be headed for the exit.

Day after day—and even in the off season, I had to

stay in top shape and be prepared. If not, the competition (individual players or teams) would take advantage of me.

VITAL PRINCIPLES

In these chapters I want to share 12 principles that have provided the foundation on which I have built my life. I like to call them "concrete shoes." In other words, they have provided a rock-solid footing for what I have been fortunate enough to accomplish.

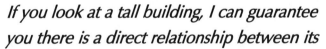

If you look at a tall building, I can guarantee you there is a direct relationship between its height and the strength of its foundation.

I believe it is vital that you have a storehouse of guiding principles, ready to use when you need them. It's like having money in the bank, you may not require your savings all at once, but it sure is nice to withdraw an amount when circumstances demand it. The rest is stored up and ready for future use.

There are times when we all come to a fork in the

road and wonder which way to turn. This is where one of the laws of life pops into mind and helps us make that crucial decision. Without this guidance we may never reach our destination.

Poole Principle #1:
Choose the Right Pattern to Follow

Every successful person I have met has a formula they followed that led to their achievement—and has kept them at the top of their profession or game.

This pattern may be an individual you chose as a role model, or a series of steps that has been proven to work.

For example, if a student wants an "A" average, he or she establishes a routine to make it happen. They say to themselves:

- "I am going to read and study."
- "I will ask plenty of questions."
- "I will be attentive in class."
- "I am going to stay organized."
- "I will not waste my time."

To maintain that "A" average requires the same ingredients—applied with even more diligence and determination. The secret is in having a game plan.

Personally, as a young man, I read the stories of professional athletes—their work habits, inner-drive, and other characteristics. Then I began to apply these attributes to my own life.

Why try to reinvent the wheel? When you discover a proven pattern for success, follow it faithfully.

Cross every "t" and dot every "i." It will shorten the road to your objective.

Poole Principle #2:
Surround Yourself With People Who are Either On the Same Level or Above You

Our family has been blessed to sit under the ministry of an outstanding preacher, Bishop Wiley Jackson of the Gospel Tabernacle Church in Atlanta. I once heard him say, "Weak people cannot help weak people."

How true. It's like the blind leading the blind.

You're going nowhere.

Sure, it's important to be compassionate when you recognize a need. But you shouldn't feel obligated to socialize continually with that individual every day and mimic their lifestyle. Instead, chose to spend a certain amount of your time guiding and showing them a better way.

It is essential to find yourself in the company of successful individuals who can elevate you to a higher level. As a result, you will be able to help even more people.

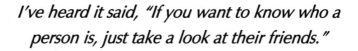

I've heard it said, "If you want to know who a person is, just take a look at their friends."

If you are the smartest person in your group, perhaps it's time to find a new set of associates. For example, if we both know how to operate a computer, I may ask a question now and again for help, or vice versa. But if you are unwilling to improve your skills, calling me constantly with trivial computer problems, that's a one-sided relationship which is robbing me of precious time.

The same would be true if you had a friend who

was struggling with a diet and calling you non-stop for support. The voice on the phone says, "Last night I couldn't help myself and wound up eating 12 donuts."

If that keeps happening, you'll eventually be thinking about food so much you are likely to put on a few extra pounds yourself!

Balance your time wisely between those who need help and those who can offer it to you.

Poole Principle #3:
Your Condition Will Remain at the Same Level as Your Confession

I've met those who are always complaining, "I'm too small," "I'm too fat," "I didn't come from the right background," "I don't have enough education"—and a dozen other excuses.

My advice is to close your mouth and stop talking that way. Your words become self-fulfilling prophecies.

The fact that I came from a humble beginning was not a hindrance to me, but a motivation to want more out of life. I did not allow my surroundings to take root and become a negative voice.

If I had spent the early years of my life saying "I'm

too short," I doubt you would be reading this book; I would have quit long ago. Instead, I looked at my circumstances totally different. If I had height, I might have become lazy and not spent hours working to improve my speed and my ability to jump.

I lifted my circumstances and my condition by raising the level of my confession.

---—»———

I declared my dreams not my deficiencies.

Walk on the Water

In addition to your own words, place a filter on what you allow others to speak into your life. When you are setting strong goals and reaching new heights, there will always be those who feel it's their duty to bring you down a notch or two.

In some cases this is pure jealousy, so consider the source. They are like crabs in a bucket. When one tries to crawl out, the others pull them back.

Many in society have a way of thinking, "Hey, you must think you are better than we are," so they will try to burst your bubble.

Be sure you fill your thoughts with *good* news instead of doom, gloom, economic collapse, and terror. The latter will only cause you to panic and will keep your eyes off the prize.

There is a story recorded in Matthew 14 of the apostle Peter who stepped out of a boat and began walking on the water toward Jesus. But when he became aware of his surroundings, listening to the howling wind and watching the angry waves, he lost his focus and started to sink. The Lord had to reach out and rescue him.

Those winds resemble the voices of the world. They'd love nothing more than to distract your attention and see you drown.

As I instill in our children at home, "The only person who can stop you is the person you look at in the mirror every day."

This is not the time to listen to negative words that spread doubt and slow your progress. Start running with the winners. Be a thoroughbred, not a donkey!

Chapter 7

Never Run From Reality

I picked up the phone and my mom was on the line. "Tyrone, can you bring our car over to grandma's house?"

"No problem," I quickly replied, trying my best not to sound too excited.

This was no small request. I was 14 years old and had never driven anywhere, except practicing with my dad—going back and forth, sticking the gears in forward and reverse, on our dirt driveway.

In LaGrange, nearly all of our relatives lived within walking distance and my grandparents were only a couple of blocks away. The streets were free of traffic, it was getting dark, and my parents decided it might be a good idea to drive home instead of walking.

This was a big deal for me. Even though I was too young for a learner's permit, my folks thought it would be safe enough for me to venture out, driving for only a minute or two.

So, feeling my oats, I climbed into the car, turned on the ignition of our used white Mercury, and backed onto our gravel street.

What Was That Noise?

I was really nervous when I turned the car onto our road. I guided the steering wheel to the left and slowly inched forward toward the stop sign ahead. When I made a right turn, I must have pulled the steering wheel too sharply because the next thing I heard was a screeching sound—like something being torn from the side of the car.

So focused on my driving, I didn't get out to look. I just wanted to deliver the car to grandma's house in one piece.

What I failed to realize was that there was a yellow fire hydrant right next to the stop sign, and I had seriously scraped it.

When I reached my destination I walked around to

the passenger side and was horrified. I thought to myself, "Tyrone, you are about to be in a heap of trouble."

My Stomach was Churning

You should have seen that car. On the passenger side, the metal trim on the panels had been torn away from the front door to the rear fender. It was just hanging off the vehicle and looked an absolute mess.

My grandparents' house was on the left hand side and the damage was on the right. So I very carefully positioned the car in a way that when my dad got in, he wouldn't see what had happened. However, I wasn't thinking straight and didn't consider the fact that my mom would have to walk around to the other side and immediately have a close-up view of what I had done.

A teenager doesn't think too clearly at a time like this.

Leaving the keys in the ignition, I quickly ran back

to our house. My stomach was churning and I was really worried. I thought, "How can I explain this away?" I had so wanted to impress my mom and dad with my driving ability.

This was the first time I ever really considered lying to my parents, but every scenario I conjured up in my mind didn't have the ring of truth.

An Unforgettable Lesson

When they returned home, my father cornered me, asking, "Son, what happened to the car?"

There was only one way out. I had to confess and own up to what I had done.

When I did, my dad really became upset. Although he didn't give me a whipping, the choice words he spoke were just as painful.

It was an unforgettable lesson.

Welcome to manhood!

Poole Principle 4:
Gas Up For Your Journey

Our journey through life isn't a 100-meter sprint,

it is a long, winding road and you had better be well prepared for the adventure. The lesson I learned at age 14 was just one of a thousand pieces of the puzzle that took me from where I was to where I was destined to be.

I can tell you from first-hand experience that if you plan to go the distance, you'd better fuel up for your journey.

If you drive from Connecticut to California, you will need more than one tank of gas. You certainly can't travel on empty.

Recharge Your Batteries

When you are busy chasing your goals, it is vital that you pay attention to any signal that indicates you are running on low, becoming weak, or depleted in strength.

There are times when it becomes absolutely essential to recharge your tired batteries and feed your mind and spirit.

For me, the best and most effective method usually involved talking with a person who had the same drive and ambition as myself—even if their ultimate goal was different than mine. There were also moments when I was inspired or recharged from an encouraging word spoken by a friend or distant relative.

Whenever I finished a conversation with a highly-motivated individual, I always left their presence with my tank overflowing. Their words kept me upbeat, focused, and reminded me of what I was trying to achieve.

Poole Principle #5:
You've Got to Maintain the Same Pressure if You Want to Maintain the Same Speed

If you expect your future to run as smooth as silk, think again. Every person experiences life's ups and downs.

For me, I knew that if I was going to rise to the top in athletics, I had to establish and maintain a strenuous work-out program.

I'll be honest, there were days when I couldn't wait to get to the gym and other times in the off-season when I tried to convince myself, "I think I'll just stay in bed this morning and work out a little harder tomorrow."

This attitude didn't cut it. I finally realized that when it was time for a workout, I had to apply the same effort to my routine regardless of how I felt at the moment.

Let me equate this to the cruise control on a car. When the vehicle is going uphill the throttle connected to the accelerator automatically kicks in so you keep the same speed and stay in the flow of traffic. Then, when you are rolling downhill, the throttle shuts down and you maintain the identical speed.

Make sure you are in complete control at all times of your own highs and lows.

STICK WITH YOUR COMMITMENT

The number one reason people fail to progress at a steady pace is their lack of self-discipline—they have goals they want to achieve, but are unable, for whatever reason, to keep a consistent schedule. Before long they're beating themself up over the problem, which leads to more failure.

Should you find yourself in this vicious cycle, take a few deep breaths, forgive yourself and get back to your routine.

To achieve success, forget your fluctuating feelings and stick with your commitment.

Make a determination to follow through regardless—rain or shine.

Always set a steady pace and never let up.

SEIZE EVERY MOMENT

Let's face it. For some, success may come easy but is hard to maintain. I know plenty of athletes who have set a personal record in a track event, but for unexplainable reasons, they couldn't repeat their feat. It was as if they congratulated themselves, and decided to live with the memory.

How do you achieve, sustain, and move on to greater and higher goals? In addition to spending time with individuals who are successful, take a close look at your targets and objectives. What will it really take to lead the field?

Whether you are in business, medicine, law, government, ministry, or education, you have the same opportunity to be in the top ten percent of your profession as any person who has ever lived. Seize every moment to move higher and higher up your chosen ladder.

Examine your work habits carefully. I certainly did. Not only did I play in the NFL 14 seasons, I started 12 of those years.

Looking back, this was only possible because I got tough on myself, kept the pressure on, and did the necessary "little things" that so many others ignored.

Perseverance pays off!

Poole Principle #6:
Raise the Bar of Learning Every Day

True education is not measured by the degree framed and hanging on your wall. I'm not impressed when I go to a doctor who graduated from John Hopkins 40 years ago. I want to know if he is keeping abreast with his specialty today.

*Learning must be a lifetime activity
that never takes a vacation.*

We live in an awesome age where information is at our fingertips and is available from so many sources. If you want an answer, just Google it!

THE INTANGIBLES

There is one truth I always keep coming back to: brains will always outdo brawn. I've seen this demonstrated over and over again.

More than once, I looked at some of the guys in the NFL and wondered, "How did he ever get here? He's not big, he's not fast, he's not strong." But you can't judge a book by its cover. It's almost impossible to accurately measure the self-confidence in a man on a mission. Passion, drive, knowledge, and personal improvement are the intangibles that separate champs from chumps.

The world will make a way for any individual who is always growing mentally, physically, and spiritually. In the words of Mike Shanahan, my coach when I was with the Denver Broncos, "If you're not improving, chances are you are not going to win."

I am a firm believer in raising the bar of learning daily. This may mean reordering your objectives and setting new goals and higher standards for yourself.

While working out at the gym is rewarding, what about your commitment to reading a certain number of books or articles each month that relate to your career or area of expertise?

It's sad to watch men and women back away from self-improvement, just when they are about to become winners. It's as if they are scared of success and, at the last minute, self-sabotage their potential. Or, they may be afraid of losing their circle of friends, or fear the responsibility that comes with being a leader.

GET READY TO STRETCH

Just as I had to face the truth when I tore the trim off the family car by hitting a fire hydrant, you have to be realistic about goal setting and raising your learning curve.

The tendency for many is to aim for a target so high that it is impossible to reach. Then when they fail they are not really very disappointed. This is the wrong approach. Always set targets that are achievable—but ones you have to stretch to reach.

Your dreams reveal your inner hidden passions, whether it is to sing on stage or be a figure skater in the Olympics. There comes a time, however, when they must no longer remain "secret" desires. You have to declare to the world what you want to accomplish, then go for it.

Never limit your dreams. Set goals for virtually every area of your life. This should include objectives for your education, finances, personal relationships, church, community, and your career.

"I Will!"

Have you ever taken the time to think long and hard about your lifetime goals? It is an exercise well worth taking. When you have completed the process, break down your game plan into 10-year, 5-year, 1-year, and 1-month goals. Now you are ready to look at priorities and what you will do today to move you closer to your ultimate target.

Along the way, perhaps circumstances will cause

you to devise a Plan B instead of Plan A. Since life is dynamic and always changing, you may need to alter your course, too.

Whatever your goals, there is absolutely nothing to fear about tomorrow, for God is already there.

Examine your vocabulary carefully. Instead of saying "I should," or "I'll try," start declaring "I will!"

I believe your dreams are about to become reality.

Chapter 8

What is Your Hot Sauce?

Not long ago I was watching a television show where the host was interviewing children. He asked one little girl, "How do you eat an elephant?"

The expected answer, of course, is, "One bite at a time."

This child, however, thought for a moment and replied, "I would eat my elephant with hot sauce."

To me, the elephant represents a gigantic problem in life. How am I going to tackle it? What steps will I have to take to solve the matter?

The usual way of overcoming a problem is trying one solution at a time. But what if the hurdle is too hard to jump over and is still there a month, a year, or five years from now? How do you keep the faith and momentum to see the issue resolved?

When I heard the young girl's answer, something clicked and I said to myself, "That's it!"

People grumble and complain, "I'm tired of broccoli," or "I hope it's not chicken again tonight!"

If chicken has become boring to your palate or is hard to digest, simply pour on your favorite flavoring—whether it's gravy, honey mustard, teriyaki, Mexican salsa, or Tabasco sauce. The right seasoning wakes up your taste buds and makes almost anything better.

For me the hot sauce mentioned by the little girl spoke of the spice of life—what motivates and gives me vision and focus. It is the secret ingredient that can overcome practically any situation.

What's Your Trigger?

As an athlete, my favorite sauce was a rigorous workout. Why? Because I knew that keeping my body in tip-top condition would help me take charge when I was on the football field.

Have you discovered a self-starting trigger that really turns you on? Perhaps it is a phrase you say when you wake up in the morning. Maybe it is how you address your first client or customer.

Is there a special something which enables you to find joy, even when you don't feel like smiling? It could be the faces of your children, or a favorite song you heard when you were a teen. Perhaps it is a particular moment in your past. Hopefully, it is your long-held dream.

———— ·》 ————

As you think about it, your senses and inner-appetite are revived and you become alive again. The adrenalin starts flowing and you are ready to tackle the world.

I hope you have found that hot sauce!

Poole Principle #7:
Defeat is a Permitted Response

When I am working out, the only music I listen to are songs that are positive and uplifting—they give me a boost of energy and get my heart pumping.

I especially enjoy the theme from a *Rocky* movie —"Eye of the Tiger." The lyrics include, "Risin' up, straight to the top...Have the guts, got the glory...Went the distance, not I'm NOT gonna stop...Just a man and his will to survive."

Every time I hear that song I can see Rocky Balboa, the "Italian Stallion," fighting as an underdog for the world boxing championship. After 15 rounds of broken noses and brutal blows, the judges' scorecards didn't really matter. The two boxers were both winners after giving the fight of their lives. There was no giving up.

You control the outcome of every experience you encounter. This is why I believe that defeat is a permitted response.

SLAM THE DOORS OF DEFEAT

It is how you handle your setbacks that determines your ultimate success. You may lose a skirmish, but you can't allow your spirit to be crushed. Instead, pick yourself up and say, "I am coming back tomorrow. There's no stopping me. I will one day taste the thrill of victory."

If you weaken your resolve and accept failure you are essentially telling yourself and the world that the enemy has defeated you and cut off your lifeline. But as long as you can keep your drive and passion alive, you are a winner-in-the-making. You have what it takes!

There are many doors that defeat loves to walk through: ignorance, laziness, procrastination, no planning, a negative attitude, and a lack of enthusiasm. However, each of these is within your power to conquer.

If your doctor tells you to lose weight and gives you a specific diet and a set of daily exercises, you have two choices. You can either follow or ignore his advice.

But if you chose to continue on your merry old way and, as a result, your body breaks down, whose fault is it? I think you know the answer. Because of your choice, you have allowed a setback.

A Helping Hand

In addition to making a decision to personally bounce back from defeat, I believe God has placed each of us on this planet to reach out to those who have lost their way and need a helping hand. We have been blessed so we can bless others.

I heard a song by the Jackson Southerneers, a legendary gospel group from Mississippi. The lyrics included these words: "Never look down on a man unless you are picking him up."

What powerful advice.

Poole Principle #8:
Examining Your Past Will Help You Understand Your Present

In one of the videos I watched of pastor Frederick Price, he made this statement: "Today will become your past and tomorrow will become your present."

How true.

Those who are on the verge of bankruptcy are at that point because of actions they took yesterday. In most cases they spent too much money, misused credit cards, and didn't pay attention to the accumulating bills. Ignoring their financial obligations led them to a crisis.

Divorce has similar roots. Somewhere in the past a

couple was looking into each other's eyes saying, "Honey, I love you." He was opening the door for her; she was cooking wonderful meals for him and it seemed like a marriage made in heaven.

Then came the jealousy, the arguments, the conflicts, the lack of communication. Suddenly, their wedding vows are forgotten, the love dies and the marriage is on the rocks.

This can be avoided by asking God to help you rekindle the flames of love that once burned so brightly.

Learn from the positive lessons of the past and leave the negative behind. This is a new day.

"That's Going to Be Me"

Goals that are not realized are nothing more than dreams and wishes. If you set an objective it should be your priority to see it through.

My dream to play professional football began very early. Starting at the age of five I would watch a game on televison, then go out in the yard and try to copy the moves of the players. I was such an ardent Dallas Cowboy fan that I could name every member of their team—offensive, defensive, and the coaches.

I can still remember watching the 1980 playoff game when the Cowboys faced Atlanta. Danny White threw a last-second pass to Drew Pearson to win the game. It was amazing, and I said to myself, "That's going to be me someday."

THE ROAD LESS TRAVELED

When I was playing high school football, there was no question that I had Division I NCAA talent, but because of my attitude at the time, such opportunities passed me by. It caused me to take a road less traveled.

However, because of the setback I experienced and the lessons I learned, when a door finally opened, I became more determined and dedicated than ever to succeed.

Regardless of the arena of life in which you play, if you fail to control the monster called pride, what you love most can be taken away.

My stubbornness and arrogance robbed me of my

senior year of high school football.

When I was kicked off the team, I didn't have a mentor to guide me on the importance of humility and how to solve the situation. I had to learn my lesson the hard way.

Now, many miles later, I am able to counsel young athletes so they won't fall into the same trap.

Poole Principle #9:
Success or Failure Doesn't "Just Happen"

It's almost impossible to reach the top of the mountain by accident. From the moment a dream is planted into your heart, you have to take steps and start moving toward it. The climb, however, is always up—which means there will be sweat and effort as you inch your way to the peak.

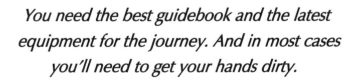

You need the best guidebook and the latest equipment for the journey. And in most cases you'll need to get your hands dirty.

If my goal is to become a carpenter, I have to learn

how to be proficient in using every tool in the toolbox. Or if my desire is to be the CEO of a high-tech firm, I'd better become an expert at every aspect of the digital world.

The same is true for those who have a vision of becoming a pro baseball or basketball player.

For me, as a defensive cornerback, I had to know the ins and outs of breaking up passes and causing fumbles.

The right tools make all the difference. If I try to eat a T-bone steak with a butter knife, I may eventually cut through the piece of meat, but it is going to require much more work on my part. In the process I might make a big mess and give up. However, if I use a sharp knife, I'll get the job done efficiently, relax, and enjoy a delicious meal.

Turn Your Future Around

Failure doesn't "just happen" either. It is the result of many factors. For example, distractions are a common cause of defeat—the wrong friends, watching too much television, a poor diet, or lack of sleep. These are the enemies of success and you need to avoid them at all cost.

Instead of floating downstream with the crowd, find a life raft and turn your future around. If you start looking, you will find someone to inspire you, an idea which sparks your creativity, an opportunity that motivates you beyond your wildest dreams.

Have you found your hot sauce?

Chapter 9

Who Controls Your Future?

At Fort Valley, I came to the realization that not every player on our team had what takes to move to the next level. Most of the guys were fun to be with, but I could tell that college sports was just a pit stop on the road of life.

While these were my friends, I had to make a tough decision regarding how I would prepare for my future. I finally came to this conclusion—even though I hesitated to say it to people face to face, my attitude was—"If you don't roll with me, then I will have to roll over you."

In other words if a person didn't have the same objective as my own, I wasn't going to allow them to hinder my progress. I faced enough self-built barriers along the way; I didn't need any coming from an outside source. Their negative influence would just make my job that much tougher.

There is a verse in the Bible that reads, "Lay aside every weight...which so easily ensnares us, and let us run with endurance the race that is set before us" (Hebrews 12:1).

To me, that meant if someone was not moving the same direction I was, they were a millstone around my neck. This "weight" had to be cut loose.

If anyone tried to discourage or talk me out of my dream I had no choice but to treat them as an opponent.

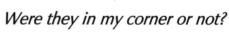

Were they in my corner or not?
Were they for me or against me?

CHASING A GOAL

By making such a move, I ran the risk that my friends would think I considered myself better than them. Not at all. I hadn't changed. It's just that there was a goal I was chasing—a place I felt I belonged—

and I didn't want anything to stand in the way.

Fortunately, there were those who saw my potential and lifted my spirits. I spent valuable time with these encouraging individuals because we had common goals and dreams. They helped me press on and move to higher ground.

This leads us to the next principle:

Poole Principle #10:
Learn to Depend on Yourself

Rising through the ranks, I had to learn many required skills "hands on." They weren't neatly laid out for me in alphabetical order. Most of the time I was on my own when it came to developing my speed and strength.

Wow! How things have changed. Today you can go to one facility and receive multi-coaching in a number of techniques. In some cases, two or three people are training one particular athlete.

That certainly wasn't my experience in college.

I really wanted to improve my agility and quickness, so my eyes lit up like a Christmas tree when I saw an ad in a publication that sells athletic equipment,

Eastbay Magazine. The ad was for platform shoes designed to help you increase speed and your vertical jump.

I read how running and sprinting takes place on the balls of your feet—and these shoes would make it possible for your heels never to touch the ground. This all sounded great to me.

A few days later, there was a package waiting at my campus post office box and I could hardly wait to open it. There they were; red and black platform shoes that would keep me on my toes.

My buddy Herman Williams and I spent many hours training in the parking lot behind the Fort Valley stadium.

IT WORKED!

I also bought a VHS videotape that demonstrated a few exercises to strengthen my Achilles, calf muscles, and quads—and I added a few drills myself.

It wasn't a waste of money to buy those shoes; they really helped me. I ran track to increase my speed, and football training developed strength. Something must have worked, because in my senior year in college, I was an NCAA All-American in both sports.

My advice to young people is to learn and apply all you can from experienced coaches, but never totally depend on their advice. There's tons of information available—and you can learn so much on your own. Yet, always make sure your goal is to be a team player, not an individual star.

Poole Principle #11:
Never Settle for Less than the Best

The summer before I entered high school I earned some spending money mowing lawns in the neighborhood. I didn't have a list of regular customers, but I took our lawn mower and a used milk container filled with gas, and went looking for grass that seemed too high. When I spotted an unruly yard, I'd knock on the door and offer my services.

My goal was to save up enough money to buy a special pair of shoes I had my heart set on. Before that time, my parents would usually pick out my shoes at Pick 'n' Pay or K-Mart. They were cheap, covered my feet, and it was all the family could afford.

So the day before my ninth grade classes began I headed for an upscale store where I had my eyes on a pair of Sebago shoes. They were extremely popular at the time and I thought owning them would really impress my friends.

With my money carefully folded in my wallet, I proudly walked into the store and showed the clerk the pair of shoes I wanted. He found my size and I tried them on. Perfect!

At the cash register, however, when he calculated the price and added the tax, my heart sank. I was a little short of cash.

Embarrassed, I walked out the door empty handed as the clerk put the shoes back on the shelf. I was really upset because what I wanted was out of my reach.

A Disaster

On the way home, I passed Pick 'n' Pay and decided to see what they had to offer. I found a pair of shoes that looked almost identical to the Sabagos, but they were definitely an off-brand.

The price met my budget, so I bought them and wore them to school the next day. However, unlike the shoes I dreamed of, which had rubber on the bottom, these were made with a hard, plastic-like material on the sole.

As I walked down the school hallway, the shoes had no grip and when I tried to stop I would slide all over the place. It was a disaster.

Right there and then, I made a decision that I would never settle for less than what I really wanted. If it took mowing a few more lawns, then that's what I would do.

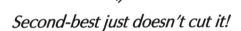

Second-best just doesn't cut it!

Wisdom from a Pro

This attitude stayed with me. When I made it to the pros, I did my best to make friends with players who were of the highest caliber. I knew they would motivate me and there was always something to learn.

In 1996, my second year with the Carolina Panthers, the team owners brought in Eric Davis from the San Francisco 49ers. He was an All-Pro who had already earned a Super Bowl ring.

Even though he was also a cornerback, I didn't consider him competition, rather a player who had much to teach me.

We became buddies and I was more than happy when he poured his wisdom as a defense player into me. He was a huge influence on my career.

Go Against the Best

Never let your ego become so inflated that you resent or fear healthy competition. The experience will only make you stronger.

The Jamaican sprinter, Usain Bolt, is a three-time World and Olympic gold medalist. As I write this he holds the all-time records in the 100-meter, 200-meter, and 4x100 meter relay. He's considered the world's fastest man.

Here is what's amazing. The sprinters who line up beside Bolt may not beat him to the finish line, but many have recorded their personal best—because he made them run faster than they would if they were against lesser competition.

I probably wouldn't make a good high school football coach because I would put the best players on the field. This probably wouldn't go over too well with a dad who donates $25,000 to the booster club to ensure his son can be in the starting lineup!

That kind of coaching is not for me.

Poole Principle #12:
Stay Focused and Never, Ever Give Up

Recently, at a speaking event, I picked a man out of the audience and asked him to come forward. With a book in my hand I told the fellow, "I want you to take this book from me."

He grabbed it and pulled, but I wouldn't let go. "Come on, take the book," I coaxed him. But the harder he pulled the more I hung on.

Finally, the guy became mad and determined enough to give it one last try. With a quick, strong tug, he snapped the book out of my grip.

The point I was trying to get across is that life can throw many curves your direction and they have a way of making you want to give up. So remember, the more obstacles that are placed in your path, the harder you have to pull.

When the world resists, you have to dig deep inside and find the energy to seize the moment and claim victory.

It Was My Choice

Every player in the pros has a reputation among his teammates and coaches. I knew from the beginning that I would never last if I went clubbing with the guys every night and neglected staying in absolutely perfect condition. It was my choice.

This attitude started in college. I wasn't about to experience another fiasco like my senior year of high school, so I became a self-starter. No one needed to tell me how hard to work or how to spend my time. Instead of going home for a lazy summer, I stayed on campus to take a few extra classes and spend as many hours as possible working out. Some days I was the only one in the room lifting weights.

I do not say this to brag, but to reemphasize how hard work pays off.

An Uncommon Commitment

When I look back at the 12 years I was a starter in

the NFL, countless players competed for my spot on every roster. During that same time there were 12 drafts and 12 free agent signing periods. But for those dozen years, I was thankful the coaches on those teams felt there was no need to replace me. I also valued the techniques and habits I acquired that contributed to my success.

Perhaps you can see why I feel such an obligation to share the knowledge I have gained with young athletes who want to help their team become champions. This training, however is not exclusive to football. It involves character development, integrity, moral standards, personal relationships, purpose, and resolve—values that create true achievement in any field of endeavor.

Most important, I tell today's youth, "Take charge of your future. Don't expect success to be handed to you on a silver platter. Ask God to give you an uncommon commitment to achieve your greatest goals."

Chapter 10

The Key to Ultimate Success

You can be blessed with all the talent in the world and develop your physical skills to their utmost, but unless you have conquered the "inside" game, life is meaningless.

The highlight moment of my career was not being a first round draft pick or wearing a Super Bowl ring. It happened in 2000 when I made a spiritual u-turn that finally allowed everything to zoom into focus.

What takes place on the field is just a blip on the screen of life. There is so much more and I wasn't the first to discover this fact. Tom Landry, who had been my hero as a coach, stated, "I'd hate to say my faith's a rock, but it's true. It is my strength; it gives me inner peace. Without my faith, I'd be in real bad shape.

Faith gives a man hope and hope is what life is all about."

The Cleansing Process

I like to compare life with a glass of water. If you fill the glass with dirty water, that's what you will be drinking. But if you find a clear spring and fill it with what is pure, everything changes.

Unfortunately, if you spend years drinking from the wrong source, it's going to take time for the impurities to flush from your system. You can't drain and refill a large pool overnight, and the greater your spiritual deficiency, the longer it will take to eliminate the pollutants. You have to pull the plug, get rid of the dirty water, turn on the spigot and refill the pool with what is clear, pure, and refreshing.

The cleansing process I am talking about involves your heart, soul, and mind. This is why the apostle Paul says, "Whatever is noble, whatever is right, whatever is pure, whatever is lovely, whatever is admirable—if anything is excellent or praiseworthy—think about such things" (Philippians 4:8).

Your thoughts control your actions.

Nourish Your Seed

If you are chasing your goal but find you are going nowhere, either you don't have the nutrients on the inside to cause the seed to grow—or you have planted the wrong seed.

In football, watching game film with the team can often be boring. So instead of biting their nails, many players chew on sunflower seeds. I've tried it, and on occasion, you bite down on a shell only to discover there is no seed inside. If that had been planted, you would reap no harvest.

Friend, God has placed within you a seed of greatness. However, if you fail to water, nourish, and cultivate the seed, it will never sprout and grow.

The Lord has done His part; now He expects you to do yours. As the Hall of Fame quarterback, Johnny Unitas observes: "There is nothing in this world that can't be accomplished through hard work and with the help of God. Don't be afraid to talk to God; after all, He is our Father."

WHAT'S REALLY IMPORTANT?

When you have a change of heart and your heavenly Father becomes the most important thing in your existence, it affects every decision you make. For example, after I was released from Indianapolis and signed by the Denver Broncos in 2001, I decided to retire from football for a year.

Everyone thought I was crazy to give up the kind of money I was making and take 12 months off. Why did I make this decision? For me it was simple. My wife, Jennifer, was giving birth to our second child and I wanted to be with them at our home in Atlanta. In other words, my family was more important than football.

The following year, however, I started in every Denver game and had one of the best seasons of my life.

A TENFOLD RETURN

Certainly there were highs and lows during my long career, but from the time I rededicated my life to the Lord, being cut from a team, or even suffering injuries, was no longer the end of my world. I had found a peace in my heart that couldn't be explained.

I could certainly identify with Steve Bartkowski, who set many records as quarterback of the Atlanta Falcons. He also had his share of setbacks and once observed, "Being benched was the lowest I've been in my life, but it was the best thing that ever happened to me. My priorities were all wrong. Football was the most important thing in my world. It was my god and I was losing my ability to handle it. Those boos totally overturned me as a person. I had to do a lot of thinking but finally I gave everything to God. He's given it back to me tenfold."

To that I say, "Amen!"

A Decision of the Heart

When I share with people about the covenant I made with God in 2000, they think there was an instant dramatic turnaround that changed me into some kind of saint. Far from it. Just as my physical life started in humble beginnings and was slowly transformed, so it has been with my spiritual walk.

I would still make some unwise decisions from time

to time, but eventually I found that my choices were lining up with the biblical principles I was learning.

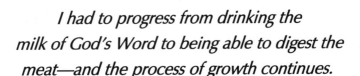

I had to progress from drinking the milk of God's Word to being able to digest the meat—and the process of growth continues.

Today, my pastor, Wiley Jackson, is a tremendous mentor and inspiration. He has helped me to reach the level where I can speak to the mountains of life and see them removed.

It is my prayer you will experience the same amazing truth I have found.

Remember:
- Choose the right pattern to follow.
- Surround yourself with people who are either on the same level or above you.
- Your condition will remain at the same level as your confession.
- Gas up for your journey.
- You've got to maintain the same pressure if you want to maintain the same speed.

- Raise the bar of learning every day.
- Defeat is a permitted response.
- Understanding your past will help you understand your future.
- Success or failure doesn't "just happen."
- Learn to depend upon yourself.
- Never settle for less than the best.
- Stay focused and never, ever give up.

Most important, examine your heart. Make certain God is at the center of every action you take. Only then will you find *Ultimate Success in the Game of Life*.

Notes

TO SCHEDULE THE AUTHOR FOR
SPECIAL EVENTS OR SPEAKING ENGAGEMENTS,
CONTACT:

TYRONE POOLE
P.O. BOX 674702
MARIETTA, GA 30067

PHONE: 770-906-6976
EMAIL: info@tyronepoole.com